P9-CCD-726

THE

WOMAN

WHO FELL

FROM THE SKY

Also by Joy Harjo

The Last Song (chapbook)

What Moon Drove Me to This?

She Had Some Horses

Secrets from the Center of the World

In Mad Love and War

Fishing (chapbook)

A Map to the Next World

W. W. NORTON & COMPANY / NEW YORK LONDON

THE

WOMAN

WHO FELL

FROM THE SKY

P O E M S

J O Y   H A R J O

Copyright © 1994 by Joy Harjo
First published as a Norton paperback 1996

All rights reserved

Printed in the United States of America

The text of this book is composed in Berling
with the display set in Charlemagne
Composition by PennSet, Inc.
Manufacturing by the Courier Companies, Inc.
Book design by Chris Welch

Library of Congress Cataloging-in-Publication Data

Harjo, Joy.
    The woman who fell from the sky : poems / Joy Harjo.
      p.   cm.
    ISBN 0-393-03715-0. — ISBN 0-393-31362-X (pbk.)
    1. Indians of North America—Poetry.   2. Indian women—Poetry.
I. Title.
PS3558.A62423W66   1996
811'.54—dc20   96–23014
                                              CIP

W. W. Norton & Company, Inc.
500 Fifth Avenue, New York, N.Y. 10110
www.wwnorton.com

W. W. Norton & Company Ltd.
Castle House, 75/76 Wells Street, London W1T 3QT

11 12 13 14 15 16 17 18 19 20

for the beautiful warriors:

my granddaughters: Krista Rae and Haleigh Sara

*my other children: Melissa, Rachelle, Ben, Megan, Karrie,
Wayne, Jason, Joseph, Angie and Jake*

and Susan M. Williams

CONTENTS

II THE WORLD ENDS HERE

MVTO

ACKNOWLEDGMENTS

With thanks to the National Endowment for the Arts and the Arizona Commission on the Arts for their support.

I'm also grateful to Pamela Uschuk and William Pitt Root for their bright presence and continued support through the everyday struggle.

And many thanks to Jill Bialosky whose faith is ever-present, to Brenda Peterson, my ally and friend for her arrangement of these works, as well as to Adrienne Rich for her generous insight, elegant wisdom.

I also acknowledge the steady and crucial assistance of Charlotte Sheedy and Bill Thompson.

And Gloria Emerson for "Wailing Jennings" in the poem "Witness."

Also thanks to the following publications: *The American Voice*; *The Best of the West 4: New Short Stories from the Wide Side of the Missouri*; *Crossroads*; *Gatherings: The En'owkin Journal of First North American Peoples*; *Hayden's Ferry Review*; *The Kenyon Review*; *New American Poets of the 90's*; *New York Times*; Oxhead Press; *Native American Literature*; *Poems for a Small Planet, A Bread Loaf Anthology*; *Sonora Review*; *The Submuloc Show/Columbus Wohs Catalogue*; *Talking Leaves*; *Talking Leaves, Contemporary Native American Short Stories*; *The Voice Literary Supplement*.

And finally to the band members of Poetic Justice: John Williams, Susan Williams, William Bluehouse Johnson, and Frank Poocha, who continue to inspire the poetry, the songs.

God is a mother, father, sister, brother, & lover

RECONCILIATION A PRAYER

I.
We gather at the shore of all knowledge as peoples who were put here by a god who wanted relatives.

This god was lonely for touch, and imagined herself as a woman, with children to suckle, to sing with—to continue the web of the terrifyingly beautiful cosmos of her womb.

This god became a father who wished for others to walk beside him in the belly of creation.

This god laughed and cried with us as a sister at the sweet tragedy of our predicament—foolish humans—

Or built a fire, as our brother to keep us warm.

This god who grew to love us became our lover, sharing tables of food enough for everyone in this whole world.

II.
Oh sun, moon, stars, our other relatives peering at us from the inside of god's house walk with us as we climb into the next century naked but for the stories we have of each other. Keep us from giving up in this land of nightmares which is also the land of miracles.

We sing our song which we've been promised has no beginning or end.

III.
All acts of kindness are lights in the war for justice.

IV.

We gather up these strands broken from the web of life. They shiver
with our love, as we call them the names of our relatives and carry
them to our home made of the four directions and sing:

Of the south, where we feasted and were given new clothes.

Of the west, where we gave up the best of us to the stars as food
for the battle.

Of the north, where we cried because we were forsaken by our
dreams.

Of the east because returned to us is the spirit of all that we love.

for the Audre Lorde Memorial 1993

THE

WOMAN

WHO FELL

FROM THE SKY

TRIBAL

MEMORY

THE CREATION STORY

I'm not afraid of love
or its consequence of light.

It's not easy to say this
or anything when my entrails
dangle between paradise
and fear.

I am ashamed
I never had the words
to carry a friend from her death
to the stars
correctly.

Or the words to keep
my people safe
from drought
or gunshot.

The stars who were created by words
are circling over this house
formed of calcium, of blood—

this house
in danger of being torn apart
by stones of fear.

If these words can do anything
I say bless this house
with stars.

Transfix us with love.

☆

There are many versions of the creation story. In one Muscogee version, the ground opened up and the people came out.

The Wind Clan people were the first to emerge. Henry Marsey Harjo, my great-grandfather, was of the Wind Clan, my great-grandmother Katie Monahwee of the Tiger Clan. Because clan association comes with one's mother, this was my grandmother Naomi Harjo's clan. She passed this clan on to my father.

This creation story lives within me and is probably the most dynamic point in the structure of my family's DNA.

THE WOMAN WHO FELL FROM THE SKY

Once a woman fell from the sky. The woman who fell from the sky was neither a murderer nor a saint. She was rather ordinary, though beautiful in her walk, like one who has experienced freedom from earth's gravity. When I see her I think of an antelope grazing the alpine meadows in mountains whose names are as ancient as the sound that created the first world.

Saint Coincidence thought he recognized her as she began falling toward him from the sky in a slow spin, like the spiral of events marking an ascension of grace. There was something in the curve of her shoulder, a familiar slope that led him into the lightest moment of his life.

He could not bear it and turned to ask a woman in high heels for a quarter. She was of the family of myths who would give everything if asked. She looked like all the wives he'd lost. And he had nothing to lose anymore in this city of terrible paradox where a woman was falling toward him from the sky.

The strange beauty in heels disappeared from the path of Saint Coincidence, with all her money held tightly in her purse, into the glass of advertisements. Saint Coincidence shuffled back onto the ice to watch the woman falling and falling.

Saint Coincidence, who was not a saint, perhaps a murderer if you count the people he shot without knowing during the stint that took his mind in Vietnam or Cambodia—remembered the girl he yearned to love when they were kids at Indian boarding school.

He could still see her on the dusty playground, off in the distance, years to the west past the icy parking lot of the Safeway. She was a blurred vision of the bittersweet and this memory had forced him to live through the violence of fire.

There they stood witness together to strange acts of cruelty by strangers, as well as the surprise of rare kindnesses.

The woman who was to fall from the sky was the girl with skinned knees whose spirit knew how to climb to the stars. Once she told him the stars spoke a language akin to the plains of her home, a language like rocks.

He watched her once make the ascent, after a severe beating. No one could touch the soul masked by name, age and tribal affiliation. Myth was as real as a scalp being scraped for lice.

Lila also dreamed of a love not disturbed by the wreck of culture she was forced to attend. It sprang up here and there like miraculous flowers in the cracks of the collision. It was there she found Johnny, who didn't have a saint's name when he showed up for school. He understood the journey and didn't make fun of her for her peculiar ways, despite the risks.

Johnny was named Johnny by the priests because his Indian name was foreign to their European tongues. He named himself Saint Co-incidence many years later after he lost himself in drink in a city he'd been sent to to learn a trade. Maybe you needed English to know how to pray in the city. He could speak a fractured English. His own language had become a baby language to him, made of the comforting voice of his grandmother as she taught him to be a human.

Johnny had been praying for years and had finally given up on a god who appeared to give up on him. Then one night as he tossed pennies on the sidewalk with his cousin and another lost traveler, he prayed to Coincidence and won. The event demanded a new name. He gave himself the name Saint Coincidence.

His ragged life gleamed with possibility until a ghost-priest brushed by him as he walked the sidewalk looking for a job to add to his stack of new luck. The priest appeared to look through to the boy in him. He despaired. He would always be a boy on his knees, the burden of shame rooting him.

Saint Coincidence went back to wandering without a home in the maze of asphalt. Asphalt could be a pathway toward God, he reasoned, though he'd always imagined the road he took with his brothers when they raised sheep as children. Asphalt had led him here to the Safeway where a woman was falling from the sky.

The memory of all time relative to Lila and Johnny was seen by an abandoned cat washing herself next to the aluminum-can bin of the grocery story.

These humans set off strange phenomena, she thought and made no attachment to the thought. It was what it was, this event, shimmering there between the frozen parking lot of the store and the sky, something unusual and yet quite ordinary.

Like the sun falling fast in the west, this event carried particles of light through the trees.

Some say God is a murderer for letting children and saints slip through his or her hands. Some call God a father of saints or a mother of demons. Lila had seen God and could tell you God was neither male nor female and made of absolutely everything of beauty, of wordlessness.

This unnameable thing of beauty is what shapes a flock of birds who know exactly when to turn together in flight in the winds used to make words. Everyone turns together though we may not see each other stacked in the invisible dimensions.

This is what Lila saw, she told Johnny once. The sisters called it blasphemy.

Johnny ran away from boarding school the first winter with his two brothers, who'd runaway before. His brothers wrapped Johnny Boy, as they called him, with their bodies to keep him warm. They froze and became part of the stars.

Johnny didn't make it home either. The school officials took him back the next day. To mourn his brothers would be to admit an unspeakable pain, so he became an athlete who ran faster than any record ever made in the history of the school, faster than the tears.

Lila never forgot about Johnny, who left school to join the army, and a few years later as she walked home from her job at Dairy Queen she made a turn in the road.

Call it destiny or coincidence—but the urge to fly was as strong as the need to push when at the precipice of any birth. It was what led her into the story told before she'd grown ears to hear, as she turned from stone to fish to human in her mother's belly.

Once, the stars made their way down stairs of ice to the earth to find mates. Some of the women were angry at their inattentive husbands, bored, or frustrated with the cycle of living and dying. They ran off with the stars, as did a few who saw their chance for travel and enlightenment.

They weren't heard from for years, until one of the women returned. She dared to look back and fell. Fell through centuries, through the beauty of the night sky, made a hole in a rock near the place Lila's mother had been born. She took up where she had left off, with her children from the stars. She was remembered.

This story was Lila's refuge those nights she'd prayed on her knees with the other children in the school dorms. It was too painful to miss her mother.

A year after she'd graduated and worked cleaning house during the day, and evenings at the Dairy Queen, she laughed to think of herself wearing her uniform spotted with sweets and milk, as she left on the arms of one of the stars. Surely she could find love in a place that did not know the disturbance of death.

While Lila lived in the sky she gave birth to three children and they made her happy. Though she had lost conscious memory of the place before, a song climbed up her legs from far away, to the rooms of her heart.

Later she would tell Johnny it was the sound of destiny, which is similar to a prayer reaching out to claim her.

You can't ignore these things, she would tell him, and it led her to the place her husband had warned her was too sacred for women.

She carried the twins in her arms as her daughter grabbed her skirt in her small fists. She looked into the forbidden place and leaped.

She fell and was still falling when Saint Coincidence caught her in his arms in front of the Safeway as he made a turn from borrowing spare change from strangers.

The children crawled safely from their mother. The cat stalked a bit of flying trash set into motion by the wave of falling—

or the converse wave of gathering together.

✮

I traveled far above the earth for a different perspective. It is possible to travel this way without the complications of NASA. This beloved planet we call home was covered with an elastic web of light. I watched in awe as it shimmered, stretched, dimmed and shined, shaped by the collective effort of all life within it. Dissonance attracted more dissonance. Harmony attracted harmony. I saw revolutions, droughts, famines and the births of new nations. The most humble kindnesses made the brightest lights. Nothing was wasted.

I understood love to be the very gravity holding each leaf, each cell, this earthy star together.

THE NAMING
FOR HALEIGH SARA BUSH

I think of names that have profoundly changed the direction of disaster. Of the raw whirling wind outlining femaleness emerging from the underworld.

It blesses the frog taking refuge under the squash-flower cloud, the stubborn weeds leaning in the direction of wind bringing rain.

My grandmother is the color of night as she tells me to move away from the window when it is storming. *The lightning will take you.*

I thought it was my long dark hair appearing as lightning. The lightning appears to be relatives.

Truth can appear as disaster in a land of things unspoken. It can be reached with white arrows, each outlining the meaning of delicate struggle.

And can happen on a night like this when the arrow light is bitten by sweet wind.

My grandmother took leave years ago by way of her aggravated heart. I haven't seen her since, but her warnings against drownings, lightning or anything else portending death by sudden means still cling to my ears.

I take those risks against the current of warnings as if she had invented negative space of wind around the curve of earth.

That night after my granddaughter-born-for-my-son climbed from the underworld we could smell ozone over the lake made of a few centuries of rain.

I went hunting for the right name and found the spirit of the ice age making plans in the bottom of the lake. Eventually the spirit will become rain, remake the shoreline with pines and laughter.

In the rain I saw the child who was carried by lightning to the other side of the storm. I saw my grandmother who never had any peace in this life blessed with animals and songs.

Oh daughter-born-of-my-son, of my grandmother, of my mother; I name you all these things:

The bag of white arrows is heavy with rain.

The earth is wet with happiness.

I never liked my mother's mother, Leona May Baker. When we would visit her and my grandfather in their two-room house in northwestern Arkansas where they were sharecroppers, she would awaken me long before dawn. I would be irritable with lack of sleep as she would sit by my bed and catalogue the gruesome details of every death of every relative and friend as well as each event of personal disaster within her known landscape.

My grandmother, who was half Cherokee and Irish, was orphaned at a very young age and raised by full-blood Cherokees in Jay, Oklahoma. She gave birth to six sons and one daughter—my mother. Each birth added to the burden of life. Once she took out a gun and shot at all of them as they ran through the trees to get away from her. My mother recalls the sounds of bullets flying by her head. My grandmother disliked my mother.

With the impending birth of my son's daughter I was prompted to find out more about this grandmother who I had never made peace with. My mother told me of her incredible gift of storytelling, how she would keep the children entranced for weeks by tales she would invent—they had no books, television or radio. And then she told me this story:

My grandfather Desmond Baker left to work on the railroad when they were especially destitute. While he was away my grandmother had an affair. When he returned nine months later she was near full term with a baby who wasn't his. He beat her until she went into labor and gave birth to the murdered child.

Shortly after the killing my grandparents attempted double suicide. They stood on the tracks while a train bore down on them as all the children watched in horror. At the last possible second my grandfather pushed my grandmother off to safety and leaped behind her.

I began to have compassion for this woman who was weighted down with seven children and no opportunities. Maybe her affair was the lightness she needed to stay alive.

When my granddaughter Haleigh was born I felt the spirit of this grandmother in the hospital room. Her presence was a blessing.

I welcomed her.

THE FLOOD

It had been years since I'd seen the watermonster, the snake who lived at the bottom of the lake. He had disappeared in the age of reason, as a mystery that never happened.

For in the muggy lake was the girl I could have been at sixteen, wrested from the torment of exaggerated fools, one version anyway, though the story at the surface would say car accident, or drowning while drinking, all of it eventually accidental.

This story is not an accident, nor is the existence of the watersnake in the memory of the people as they carried the burden of the myth from Alabama to Oklahoma. Each reluctant step pounded memory into the broken heart and no one will ever forget it.

When I walk the stairway of water into the abyss, I return as the wife of the watermonster, in a blanket of time decorated with swatches of cloth and feathers from our favorite clothes.

The stories of the battles of the watersnake are forever ongoing, and those stories soaked into my blood since infancy like deer gravy, so how could I resist the watersnake, who appeared as the most handsome man in the tribe, or any band whose visits I'd been witness to since childhood?

This had been going on for centuries: the first time he appeared I carried my baby sister on my back as I went to get water. She laughed at a woodpecker flitting like a small sun above us and before I could deter the symbol we were in it.

My body was already on fire with the explosion of womanhood as if I were flint, hot stone, and when he stepped out of the water he was the first myth I had ever seen uncovered. I had surprised him in a human moment. I looked aside but I could not discount what I had seen.

My baby sister's cry pinched reality, the woodpecker a warning of a disjuncture in the brimming sky, and then a man who was not a man but a myth.

What I had seen there were no words for except in the sacred language of the most holy recounting, so when I ran back to the village, drenched in salt, how could I explain the water jar left empty by the river to my mother who deciphered my burning lips as shame?

My imagination swallowed me like a mica sky, but I had seen the watermonster in the fight of lightning storms, breaking trees, stirring up killing winds, and had lost my favorite brother to a spear of the sacred flame, so certainly I would know my beloved if he were hidden in the blushing skin of the suddenly vulnerable.

I was taken with a fever and nothing cured it until I dreamed my fiery body dipped in the river where it fed into the lake. My father carried me as if I were newborn, as if he were presenting me once more to the world, and when he dipped me I was quenched, pronounced healed.

My parents immediately made plans to marry me to an important man who was years older but would provide me with everything I needed to survive in this world, a world I could no longer perceive, as I had been blinded with a ring of water when I was most in need of a drink by a snake who was not a snake, and how did he know my absolute secrets, those created at the brink of acquired language?

When I disappeared it was in a storm that destroyed the houses of my relatives; my baby sister was found sucking on her hand in the crook of an oak.

And though it may have appeared otherwise, I did not go willingly. That night I had seen my face strung on the shell belt of my ancestors, and I was standing next to a man who could not look me in the eye.

The oldest woman in the tribe wanted to remember me as a symbol in the story of a girl who disobeyed, who gave in to her desires before marriage and was destroyed by the monster disguised as the seductive warrior.

Others saw the car I was driving as it drove into the lake early one morning, the time the carriers of tradition wake up, before the sun or the approach of woodpeckers, and found the emptied six-pack on the sandy shores of the lake.

The power of the victim is a power that will always be reckoned with, one way or the other. When the proverbial sixteen-year-old woman walked down to the lake within her were all sixteen-year-old women who had questioned their power from time immemorial.

Her imagination was larger than the small frame house at the north edge of town, with the broken cars surrounding it like a necklace of futility, larger than the town itself leaning into the lake. Nothing could stop it, just as no one could stop the bearing-down thunderheads as they gathered overhead in the war of opposites.

Years later when she walked out of the lake and headed for town, no one recognized her, or themselves, in the drench of fire and rain. The watersnake was a story no one told anymore. They'd entered a drought that no one recognized as drought, the convenience store a signal of temporary amnesia.

I had gone out to get bread, eggs and the newspaper before breakfast and hurried the cashier for my change as the crazy woman walked in, for I could not see myself as I had abandoned her some twenty years ago in a blue windbreaker at the edge of the man-made lake as everyone dove naked and drunk off the sheer cliff, as if we had nothing to live for, not then or ever.

It was beginning to rain in Oklahoma, the rain that would flood the world.

Embedded in Muscogee tribal memory is the creature the tie snake, a huge snake of a monster who lives in waterways and will do what he can to take us with him. He represents the power of the underworld.

He is still present today in the lakes and rivers of Oklahoma and Alabama, a force we reckon with despite the proliferation of inventions that keep us from ourselves.

A POSTCOLONIAL TALE

Every day is a reenactment of the creation story. We emerge from dense unspeakable material, through the shimmering power of dreaming stuff.

This is the first world, and the last.

Once we abandoned ourselves for television, the box that separates the dreamer from the dreaming. It was as if we were stolen, put into a bag carried on the back of a whiteman who pretends to own the earth and the sky. In the sack were all the people of the world. We fought until there was a hole in the bag.

When we fell we were not aware of falling. We were driving to work, or to the mall. The children were in school learning subtraction with guns, although they appeared to be in classes.

We found ourselves somewhere near the diminishing point of civilization, not far from the trickster's bag of tricks.

Everything was as we imagined it. The earth and stars, every creature and leaf imagined with us.

The imagining needs praise as does any living thing. Stories and songs are evidence of this praise.

The imagination conversely illumines us, speaks with us, sings with us.

Stories and songs are like humans who when they laugh are indestructible.

No story or song will translate the full impact of falling, or the inverse power of rising up.

Of rising up.

✮

*The landscape of the late twentieth century is littered with bodies of our
relatives. Native peoples in this country were 100 percent of the popula-
tion a few hundred years ago. We are now one half of 1 percent. Vio-
lence is a prevalent theme in the history of this land.*

*I think of the death of the brother of a Dakota friend of mine who was
killed recently in Oakland. When a program to inspire the creativity of
Indian children lost funding and couldn't pay him for his services he
kept working out of commitment and love for these children. His killing
was a reckless act by other Indian men who were just over the legal defi-
nition of the age of childhood, who did not even know him.*

*As I write this I am interrupted by an Apache man who is passing by
my table in a restaurant owned by his tribe. He asks me first about my
portable computer, then tells me he has come home to bury his son, who
was shot and killed because he intercepted some young men who were
partying on the street in front of his home in a place not far from Oak-
land. He, his wife and daughter-in-law have brought him home to bury
him.*

*Their grief is slick with tears that will be soaked up by this beautiful
land.*

*If I am a poet who is charged with speaking the truth (and I believe the
word* poet *is synonymous with truth-teller), what do I have to say about
all of this?*

MOURNING SONG

It's early evening here in the small world, where gods gamble for good weather as the sky turns red. Oh grief rattling around in the bowl of my skeleton. How I'd like to spit you out, turn you into another human, or remake the little dog spirit who walked out of our house without its skin toward an unseen land. We were left behind to figure it out during a harvest turned to ashes. I need to mourn with the night, turn to the gleaming house of bones under your familiar brown skin. The hot stone of our hearts will make a fire. If we cry more tears we will ruin the land with salt; instead let's praise that which would distract us with despair. Make a song for death, a song with yellow teeth and bad breath. For loneliness, the house guest who eats everything and refuses to leave. A song for bad weather so we can stand together under our leaking roof, and make a terrible music with our wise and ragged bones.

In the city in which I live are many homeless people. They congregate near the post office and coffeehouse I frequent. I've gotten to know one woman by name, though another woman terrifies me with her quiet insanity. I make a wide circle around her and feel guilty every time I see her. I'm especially disturbed when I see my Indian relatives suffering such a loss. Often they are the very tribe whose land is now called Albuquerque.

Because my family has suffered from the destruction of alcohol, as have most Indian families in this land, I don't want to encourage the drinking with spare change, but I also understand the need to deaden the pain. It's a quandary I haven't settled.

Once far down the sidewalk I spotted two Indian men who were asking passersby for money. I tried to make myself invisible so I wouldn't have to confront the pain, but they saw me anyway. I was shocked to recognize my old friend, a tall good-looking Navajo who always had a good story.

He was filthy, his hair thick with lice. He also recognized me and couldn't let it pass that I had gained some weight since my svelte twenties! We laughed and hugged each other, then cried.

I am still thinking of him and how each of us chooses our path daily, though our choices often appear limited by race, sex and class.

Knowing him the way I did I couldn't help but think he'd made a choice to be a modern warrior, and could gather more crucial knowledge from the streets of this city than he could have on a track called success by the colonizers.

NORTHERN LIGHTS

Northern lights were sighted above Lake Superior as we danced concentric circles around the drums at Ashland, each step bringing us through the freezing. Bells, the occasional sacred flute and the drum marking more than time, rather outlining ancestors or a pipeline into the earth to the mother of volcanoes.

I noticed Whirling Soldier beneath the garish lights of the auditorium. He trusted nothing, still broke swords with angry gods. His war scars were evident in the way his eyes flinched and burned with gunpowder, from the recurring horror of his decapitated ditchmate draped on the trees, spilled across him.

We talked wild rice, modern fiction and of his daughter hitting eighteen sober after drinking away adolescence. We were proud to watch her dance by us, her eyes on fire with the intimate knowledge of survival from the abyss. She carried her niece, his granddaughter, who was laughing to see so many grandmothers, so many relatives.

He had returned from the war, from Wichita with a spirit feather pressed against his heart. The killing wind chafed his lips. There were no prayers anymore. All he knew was he was leaving Nam, and approaching the destruction of his people by laws.

The northern lights were reminiscent of mercy gathering on the horizon. Sometimes he thought he saw them in Nam, or was it fire from the unseen enemy, which could have come from the boy from Ohio in the foxhole next to him, or the gook rattling the bush who appeared as his cousin Ralph, an apparition making an offering of the newest crop of wild rice?

He was killing himself he thought; each shot rigged his spine to hell. There was no way to get out, he was in it, and knew the warrior code said nothing about the wailing of children in the dark. The sacrifice reminded him of his mother stuffing wood into the stove, cooking potatoes in the grey before dawn, before she went to clean houses. They never had enough to eat. He always looked for his father instead of going to school with his sisters, his stomach warm with potatoes and coffee, sometimes fresh deer meat when they were lucky.

Suddenly he was in Vietnam, a man as his father had been when he had found him floating on ice in the lake. His father had been fishing for redemption when his heart gave out. His empty bottle skudded away, slipped into the river, an epitaph read by fish drinking in the lake.

Under fire the image of his father on ice often took hold through the scope and his teeth would chatter in the hot, damp jungle as if he were freezing, but he couldn't put his rifle down. And nothing killed the image, kept it from growing on its own.

Soon it was spring and the lake thawed and his father sank to the bottom. Deer stopped to drink. Clouds surfaced in the blue. Whirling Soldier made it through summer, then was shot clean through. The bullet missed the shinbone while he was flying on heroin making volcanoes of the bush.

By then he couldn't see through to the surface of the lake. He was lucky to be able to walk, climb up the muddy bank, make it to Wichita after the blur of San Francisco, Oklahoma City on his way home.

In Yuma, in the hangover of a dream of his mother beading a blanket in his honor he tore the medals from his pack and pawned them for a quart. He snuffed his confusion between honor and honor with wine, became an acrobat of pain in the Indian bars of Kansas.

One of those mornings, no different from any other except for the first taste of winter, reminded him of the beginning of the world and he imagined his mother wrapping a deer-meat sandwich in a plastic bread wrapper. When he opened the door his breath took the form of question marks, imitated clouds over water. His father sat up on the sagging bed, coughed, asked him where he was going. But he didn't hear the question until years later, as he staggered up some state road north of Wichita, with a pint of Seagram's tucked in his pants, the staccato of machine gun still stuttering in his memory.

What must have been the head crow laughed from a stiff telephone wire, swang back and forth beneath the sun, blinking his eyes at the sleeping pitiful world.

Whirling Soldier muttered, his voice broke off in waves. He wished he had a cigarette. The eye of a dried sunflower reminded him his baby would be two, but she too had probably disappeared in the azimuth of forgetfulness. He unscrewed the cap of his final fix.

His last fight did not involve the clockwork of artillery but a punch that shattered the mouth of a man who looked like his brother. He staggered away from the shiny blood pool, and threw up in the weeds breaking the sidewalk. Suddenly, the high winds of violence that chased him from fight to fight found him north of Wichita, at dawn, talking to a spirit who had never been a stranger but a relative he'd never met.

I can't tell you what took place beneath the blessing sun for the story doesn't belong to me but to Whirling Soldier, who gifted me with it in the circle of hope. After the dance we all ran out onto the ice to see the northern lights. They were shimmering relatives returned from the war, dancing in the skies all around us. It was an unusual moment of grace for fools.

☆

I was invited up north once to a small college off Lake Superior. The events of the week culminated in a community powwow. This was the highlight of my visit. I felt honored to be part of the circle, with the drum as the heartbeat and the songs lifting us up to the sky together.

A young Ojibwa woman just past eighteen who had just begun to write poetry as one of her efforts to save her life introduced me to her father, who was also a writer. As we stood in the circle, the people dancing by us he gifted me with a tale about a man who had lost everything to the ravages of war on this continent and in Vietnam, yet survived the many deaths.

If I were to tell the story no one would believe me. The power of it almost destroyed a man and his family, yet was also their survival.

WHO INVENTED DEATH AND CROWS AND IS THERE ANYTHING WE CAN DO TO CALM THE NOISY CLATTER OF DESTRUCTION?

What a hard year. We're all dying, even that crow talking loud and kicking up snow.

Maybe he thinks he can head it off with a little noise, a fight. Or his silver-colored soul just wants some attention in his feathered suit.

That's what I like about crows. Decorum has another shape. They aren't afraid to argue about the inarguable.

We fly into the body and we fly out, changed by the sun, by crows who manipulate the borders of reason.

Of course it's not that easy, and I'm circumventing the matter as I marvel at the sun sleeping in the snow—

the talk of crows getting in the way of poetry. I have a question for my soul, a creature who has little patience with crows—and less with snow.

This question grows new leaves with each hard rain yet bends with grief at loss in the cold.

This morning the question gleams with particles of the sun. There's crying; there's laughter.

What do you make of it?

☆

When I hear crows talking, death is a central topic. Death often occurs in clusters, they say. They watch the effect like a wave that moves out from the center of the question. The magnetic force is attractive and can make you want to fly to the other side of the sky.

THE MYTH OF BLACKBIRDS

The hours we counted precious were blackbirds in the density of
Washington. Taxis toured the labyrinth with passengers of mist as
the myth of ancient love took the shape of two figures carrying
the dawn tenderly on their shoulders to the shores of the
Potomac.

We fled the drama of lit marble in the capitol for a refuge held up
by sweet, everlasting earth. The man from Ghana who wheeled our
bags was lonesome for his homeland, but commerce made it neces-
sary to carry someone else's burdens. The stars told me how to find
us in this disorder of systems.

Washington did not ever sleep that night in the sequence of eternal
nights. There were whirring calculators, computers stealing names,
while spirits of the disappeared drank coffee at an all-night café in
this city of disturbed relativity.

Justice is a story by heart in the beloved country where imagination
weeps. The sacred mountains only appear to be asleep. When we fi-
nally found the room in the hall of mirrors and shut the door I
could no longer bear the beauty of scarlet licked with yellow on the
wings of blackbirds.

This is the world in which we undressed together. Within it white
deer intersect with the wisdom of the hunter of grace. Horses wheel
toward the morning star. Memory was always more than paper and
cannot be broken by violent history or stolen by thieves of child-
hood. We cannot be separated in the loop of mystery between
blackbirds and the memory of blackbirds.

And in the predawn when we had slept for centuries in a drenching sweet rain you touched me and the springs of clear water beneath my skin were new knowledge. And I loved you in this city of death.

Through the darkness in the sheer rise of clipped green grass and asphalt our ancestors appear together at the shoreline of the Potomac in their moccasins and pressed suits of discreet armor. They go to the water from the cars of smokey trains, or dismount from horses dusty with fatigue.

See the children who became our grandparents, the old women whose bones fertilized the corn. They form us in our sleep of exhaustion as we make our way through this world of skewed justice, of songs without singers.

I embrace these spirits of relatives who always return to the place of beauty, whatever the outcome in the spiral of power. And I particularly admire the tender construction of your spine which in the gentle dawning is a ladder between the deep in which stars are perfectly stars, and the heavens where we converse with eagles.

And I am thankful to the brutal city for the space which outlines your limber beauty. To the man from Ghana who also loves the poetry of the stars. To the ancestors who do not forget us in the concrete and paper illusion. To the blackbirds who are exactly blackbirds. And to you sweetheart as we make our incredible journey.

☆

I believe love is the strongest force in this world, though it doesn't often appear to be so at the ragged end of this century.

And its appearance in places of drought from lovelessness is always startling.

Being in love can make the connections between all life apparent—

whereas lovelessness emphasizes the absence of relativity.

THE SONG OF THE HOUSE IN THE HOUSE

I've seen a ghost house in the street
loom up behind a man with lice wearing a blanket
who was someone I loved, a father or a brother.

Do you know how it is to hold on to anything in the dark,
said the man who was the child of unspoken wishes
rattling the toys in the ghost house?

The velocity of fear overtakes the spin of a warring planet,
and the scent of urine reminds the house of the child in diapers
who fell asleep to the sound of his mother rustling
the sheets while evil took a turn in the house.

The sound emphasized songlessness
of a mother who could not watch and turned on the
television. She slept and slept while
the children grew in the house that slanted
toward the thing devouring it.

There's no easy way to know this thing, said the man
who grew smaller in the shadow of the house as it leaned over
to smell the tender neck of the child as he sipped
wine with other strangers.

When the earth makes a particularly hard turn
someone can fall off—a house can tilt
toward the street or ride the hip of destruction.

To maneuver deftly can mean learning another angle
of motion to take the place of wine
and other spirits caught by shiny glass or powder
attracted by the wound of those who once knew how to sing.

I'm sorry, said the house who sat down by the man
who'd taken refuge in the street.

The inhabitants could be heard disappearing
through aluminum walls as the boy bent
to the slap and beating by the father who was charged
with loving and nothing in him could answer to that angel.

I could not protect you, cried the house:

Though the house gleamed with appliances.
Though the house was built with postwar money
and hope.
Though the house was their haven after the war.
Though the war never ended.

☆

*I believe an architectural structure is interactive. The elements of con-
struction: adobe, lumber, glass, steel and fabric are living. We don't just
live in a house, but with it.*

*The houses and rooms in which we live and lived stay with us. Hopes
and dreams are buried in them, as are cries of love and the bruises of
violence.*

*If a particular house or room is crucial to our understanding love, that
place too grows attached to us, misses us.*

INSOMNIA AND THE SEVEN STEPS TO GRACE

At dawn the panther of the heavens peers over the edge of the world. She hears the stars gossip with the sun, sees the moon washing her lean darkness with water electrified by prayers. All over the world there are those who can't sleep, those who never awaken.

My granddaughter sleeps on the breast of her mother with milk on her mouth. A fly contemplates the sweetness of lactose.

Her father is wrapped in the blanket of nightmares. For safety he approaches the red hills near Thoreau. They recognize him and sing for him.

Her mother has business in the house of chaos. She is a prophet disguised as a young mother who is looking for a job. She appears at the door of my dreams and we put the house back together.

Panther watches as human and animal souls are lifted to the heavens by rain clouds to partake of songs of beautiful thunder.

Others are led by deer and antelope in the wistful hours to the villages of their ancestors. There they eat cornmeal cooked with berries that stain their lips with purple while the tree of life flickers in the sun.

It's October, though the season before dawn is always winter. On the city streets of this desert town lit by chemical yellow travelers search for home.

Some have been drinking and intimate with strangers. Others are escapees from the night shift, sip lukewarm coffee, shift gears to the other side of darkness.

One woman stops at a red light, turns over a worn tape to the last chorus of a whispery blues. She has decided to live another day.

The stars take notice, as do the half-asleep flowers, prickly pear and chinaberry tree who drink exhaust into their roots, into the earth.

She guns the light to home where her children are asleep and may never know she ever left. That their fate took a turn in the land of nightmares toward the sun may be untouchable knowledge.

It is a sweet sound.

The panther relative yawns and puts her head between her paws. She dreams of the house of panthers and the seven steps to grace.

☆

I think of Bell's theorem which states that all actions have a ripple effect in this world. We could name this theorum for any tribe in this country as tribal peoples knew this long before we knew English or the scientific method.

One middle of the night when it was hot in Tucson and I couldn't sleep, I imagined the ripple as it began in that small studio and radiated out and back again.

LETTER FROM THE END
OF THE TWENTIETH CENTURY

I shared a half hour of my life this morning with Rammi, an Igbo man from northern Nigeria who drove me in his taxi to the airport. Chicago rose up as a mechanical giant with soft insides buzzing around to keep it going. We were part of the spin.

Rammi told the story of his friend, who one morning around seven —a morning much like this one—was filling his taxi with gas. He was imagining home, a village whose memories had given him sustenance to study through his degree and would keep him going one more year until he had the money he needed to return.

As the sun broke through the grey morning he heard his mother tell him, the way she had told him when he was a young boy, how the sun had once been an Igbo and returned every morning to visit relatives.

These memories were the coat that kept him warm on the streets of ice.

He was interrupted by a young man who asked him for money, a young man who was like many he saw on his daily journey onto the street to collect fares. "Oh no, sorry man. I don't have anything I can give you," he said as he patted the pockets of his worn slacks, his thin nylon jacket. He saved every penny because he knew when he returned he'd be taking care of his family, a family several houses large.

He turned back to the attention of filling his gas tank. What a beautiful morning, almost warm. And the same sun, the same Igbo looking down on him in the streets of the labyrinth far far from home.

And just like that he was gone, from a gunshot wound at the back of his head—the hit of a casual murderer.

As we near the concrete plains of O'Hare, I imagine the spirit of Rammi's friend at the door of his mother's house, the bag of dreams in his hands dripping with blood. His mother's tears make a river of red stars to an empty moon.

The whole village mourns with her. The ritual of tears and drums summon the ancestors who carry his spirit into the next world. There he can still hear the drums of his relatives as they accompany him on his journey. He must settle the story of his murder before joining his ancestors or he will come back a ghost.

The smallest talking drum is an insistent heart, leads his spirit to the killer, a young Jamaican immigrant who was traced to his apartment because his shirt of blood was found by the police, thrown off in the alley with his driver's license in the pocket.

He searches for his murderer in the bowels of Chicago and finds him shivering in a cramped jail cell. He could hang him or knife him—and it would be called suicide. It would be the easiest thing.

But his mother's grief moves his heart. He hears the prayers of the young man's mother. There is always a choice, even after death.

He gives the young man his favorite name and calls him his brother. The young killer is then no longer shamed but filled with remorse and cries all the cries he has stored for a thousand years. He learns to love himself as he never could, because his enemy, who has every reason to destroy him, loves him.

That's the story that follows me everywhere and won't let me sleep: from Tallahassee Grounds to Chicago, to my home near the Rio Grande.

It sustains me through these tough distances.

I was in a downtown Chicago hotel room when I called home, as I do every morning and evening when I am away—and was shocked by the story of an Albuquerque taxi driver who was stabbed in the neighborhood I had just moved from a few weeks before. The driver dragged himself to the porch of a home that may have been the house that had been sweet harbor for us, to call for help. He died there.

I knew many of the taxi drivers because I often took a taxi to the airport. I fearfully imagined the faces and voices of all of them.

I could smell this tragedy though I was far away from home. I imagined being able to do something had I been there, instead I was throwing up as I imagined washing his blood off my porch, calling his relatives. Did he have a daughter? Or sons? Who told his mother and how would she bury him?

That morning I took a taxi from the hotel to O'Hare with a taxi driver who introduced himself to me as "Rammi." I was still shaken with the story of the death of the Albuquerque taxi driver. I have no explanation for senseless acts of violence. The weight was pressing me.

Rammi and I began talking. As an Indian woman in this country I often find I have much in common with many of the immigrants from other colonized lands who come here to make a living, often as taxi drivers. He told me of his friend, another taxi driver who was killed in similar circumstances as the Albuquerque driver.

THE WORLD

ENDS HERE

WITNESS

I walk the streets of a town in Italy. At night the walls of the amphi-
theater flutter with shadows of lions and Christians. The four gates
of power appear languid as off-duty angels.

We can walk through walls eventually by faith and could all along,
as misty forms passing through myths no one would ever believe:
the tragic heroine becomes the trickster caught in the circle of ob-
scenity becomes the woman who after pulling in her laundry from a
window adjusts her bra strap. It is the only gesture in the world.

Every street leads to the center of town, which is an imaginary
house with a table set for fools. The newly dead lean at the win-
dows, caught by the clatter of knives and forks, the talk of ordinary
things.

This is why they weep and are who we mistake for the wind when
we are grabbing at the blankets as we slide into waves of sleep. No
lover can suspend that loneliness.

We approached the tower sheltered by perpetual oaks. The Guinigi
family will disappear if the magic isn't watered, so the roots are
soaked and water makes a pool at my feet.

Or is it the shadow of a woman on the run?

They discovered her decomposed body in the fields near her hus-
band's pueblo ten years ago, on a night like this one. She put her ear
to the ground and ran shoulder first into the earth. Turquoise was
stripped from her ears.

I taste the same wind. The stars were witness. I have seen them
above us as sisters, her escort to another life, though tragedy would
place them behind an eclipsed moon searching the alleys for scraps
of food.

I can smell spring everywhere as it erupts in the bowels of death. My leg bones know they are sticks for plants that will be watered by blood.

It was during the revolution, a night like this one when you can put your arms over the shoulders of the closest stars and laugh together. The moon wore a Stetson of water.

Someone else we loved lost hope and smashed their car into a wall that wasn't there. The reports said they were drinking. I nearly lost it myself a few times in the days of the angry count.

Once, we were driving the back roads around Albuquerque, the radio on country and a six-pack. It wasn't me flipping the tabs as we traded one-word jokes in Navajo, but I have remembered the story so often that I will always ride with her in the careening truck.

Soon there were sirens, turning lights and she pulled to a stop at the side of the road. Damn the cops. She rolled down the window, wailing Jennings tearing up the cab. They cited her for weaving! (She came from a family renowned for weaving.)

We laughed and laughed. And the laughter resurrected the lost ones two-stepping in the Bandbox Bar, where we had danced those nights we thought we had lost everything, heard the stabbings outside the door.

Around midnight the puppet maker appears exactly in time, in a room of whitewashed adobe, the only light on in Lucca. He thinks no one is watching as he dances with a puppet who is the memory of a lover he once walked the street with as a voyeur of the infinitely beautiful. An Italian libretto provides the curve.

The walls constructed for defense around the town turn to grass. He laughs and cries to himself, remembering everything.

✩

The Indian wars never ended in this country. We could date them as beginning with contact by Columbus, an Italian hired by the Spanish court to find the land of spice and gold. Of course we fought intertribally and among ourselves, but a religious fervor large enough to nearly destroy a continent was imported across the Atlantic.

We were hated for our difference by our enemies.

The civil rights movement awakened many of us to the beauty in our difference. We began to understand how oppression had become our eyes, our ears, our tongues—we rose up together and continued to sing, as we always had, but with more pride, a greater love for ourselves.

We were energetic with our remembered love and stood with each other. The tragedies of loss and heartbreak appeared even more terrible at this time.

During this reawakening I remember being in the thick of plans for the new world: in coffeehouses, in the pine smell of mountain retreats, on the road. We are still working on them.

WOLF WARRIOR

FOR ALL THE WARRIORS

A white butterfly speckled with pollen joined me in my prayers yesterday as I thought of you in Washington. I didn't want the pain of repeated history to break your back. In my blanket of hope I walked with you, wolf warrior and the council of tribes, to what used to be the Department of War to discuss justice.

(When a people institute a bureaucratic department to serve justice then be suspicious. False justice is not justified by massive structure, just as the sacred is not confineable to buildings constructed for the purpose of worship.)

I pray these words don't obstruct the meaning I am searching to give you, a gift like love so you can approach that strange mind without going insane. So we can all walk with you, sober, our children empowered with the clothes of memory in which they are never hungry for love, or justice.

An old Cherokee who prizes wisdom above the decisions rendered by departments of justice told me this story. It isn't Cherokee but a gift given to him from the people in the north. I know I carried this story for a reason and now I understand I am to give it to you.

A young man, about your age or mine, went camping with his dogs. It was just a few years ago, not long after the eruption of Mount St. Helens, when white ash covered the northern cities, an event predicting a turning of the worlds.

I imagine October and bear's fat with berries of the brilliant harvest, before the freezing breath of the north settles in and the moon is easier to reach by flight without planes.

His journey was a journey toward the unknowable, and that night as he built a fire out of twigs and broken boughs he remembered the thousand white butterflies climbing toward the sun when he had camped there last summer.

Dogs were his beloved companions in the land that had chosen him through the door of his mother. His mother continued to teach him well and it was she who had reminded him that the sound of pumping oil wells might kill him, turn him toward money.

So he and his dogs traveled out into the land that remembered everything, including butterflies, and the stories that were told when light flickered from grease.

That night as he boiled water for coffee and peeled potatoes he saw a wolf walking toward camp on her hind legs. It had been a generation since wolves had visited his people. The dogs were awed to see their ancient relatives and moved over to make room for them at the fire. The lead wolf motioned for her companions to come with her and they approached humbly, welcomed by the young man who had heard of such goings on but the people had not been so blessed since the church had fought for their souls.

He did not quite know the protocol, but knew the wolves as relatives and offered them coffee, store meat and fried potatoes which they relished in silence. He stoked the fire and sat quiet with them as the moon in the form of a knife for scaling fish came up and a light wind ruffled the flame.

The soundlessness in which they communed is what I imagined when I talked with the sun yesterday. It is the current in the river of your spinal cord that carries memory from sacred places, the sound of a thousand butterflies taking flight in windlessness.

He knew this meeting was unusual and she concurred, then told the story of how the world as they knew it had changed and could no longer support the sacred purpose of life. Food was scarce, pups were being born deformed and their migrations which were in essence a ceremony for renewal were restricted by fences. The world as all life on earth knew it would end and there was still time in the circle of hope to turn back the destruction.

That's why they had waited for him, called him here from the town a day away over the rolling hills, from his job constructing offices for the immigrants.

They shared a smoke and he took the story into his blood, while the stars nodded their heads, while the dogs murmured their agreement. "We can't stay long," the wolf said. "We have others with whom to speak and we haven't much time."

He packed the wolf people some food to take with them, some tobacco and they prayed together for safety on this journey. As they left the first flakes of winter began falling and covered their tracks. It was as if they had never been there.

But the story burned in the heart of this human from the north and he told it to everyone who would listen, including my elder friend who told it to me one day over biscuits and eggs.

The story now belongs to you too, and much as pollen on the legs of a butterfly is nourishment carried by the butterfly from one flowering to another, this is an ongoing prayer for strength for us all.

☆

One morning I prepared to see a friend off to Washington, D.C., to argue a tribe's right to water. The first time I visited there I suffered from vertigo and panic attacks. I saw rivers of blood flowing under the beautiful white marble monuments that announced power in the landscape. I knew of the history embedded in the city. All tribes in this country have sharp memories located here. My great-great-grandfather Monahwee went there with other tribal members to conduct business on behalf of the tribe. Those concerns have never been settled.

It was early summer and my garden was growing well, especially due to the efforts of a white butterfly who greeted me each morning. I watched her work and for the first time in my life realized how deeply important were the efforts of this creature. I was easily aware of the need for sun and rain, but the butterfly's job was just as crucial. She always showed up in time. I wondered who assigned her to our particular garden.

The butterfly's presence shifted the meaning of that summer as did a story told to me by Bob Thomas, a Cherokee scholar who had been a colleague of mine at the University of Arizona. He had just returned from a conference for native elders somewhere in the far north where a young man from one of those northern tribes, Inuit or Athabascan, approached him with a story, a story the wolves had recently given him with a sense of urgency.

I believe in the power of words to create the world, as did the wolves who told that story to the young man, as did Bob Thomas who told me the story, and my friend who took this story with her and the tribe to Washington, D.C.

PROMISE OF BLUE HORSES

A blue horse turns into a streak of lightning,
                                    then the sun—
relating the difference between sadness
                                    and the need to praise
that which makes us joyful. I can't calculate
                                    how the earth tips hungrily
toward the sun—then soaks up rain—or the density
                                    of this unbearable need
to be next to you. It's a palpable thing—this earth philosophy—
                                    and familiar in the dark
like your skin under my hand. We are a small earth. It's no
                                    simple thing. Eventually
we will be dust together, can be used to make a house, to stop
                                    a flood or grow food
for those who will never remember who we were, or know
                                    that we loved fiercely.
Laughter and sadness eventually become the same song turning us
                                    toward the nearest star—
a star constructed of eternity and elements of dust barely visible
                                    in the twilight as you travel
east. I run with the blue horses of electricity who surround
                                    the heart
and imagine a promise made when no promise was possible.

The heart is constructed of a promise to love. As it distributes the blood
of memory and need through the body its song reminds us of the promise
—a promise that is electrical in impulse and radiation.

SONATA FOR THE INVISIBLE

FOR MY SON

We are comfortable on the rich grass stolen from arid beauty, and watch the sun beat on an ensemble of singers and dancers from a horse people from the north who aren't used to the heat.

They illustrate different dances to the crowd, who were fooled into thinking there's nothing left, but songs are a cue as to what walks among us unseen.

Ancestors stand with jackrabbit and saguaro—all of us beneath the flight of dipping hawks.

The drum makes a wedge into consciousness before the flute player begins melodic flight on notes based on a scale that has nothing to do with the construction of a piano in Europe.

This scale involves the relationship of the traveler's horse to the morning star and what the arc makes as it lovingly re-creates red dawn.

Somewhere far from here it is raining as steady as the pattern the grass makes and it has been raining hard for years.

The hawk makes an elegant scribble in the wing of mist and within this story is the flute player who acquires the secret of flying.

I hear the opening of the Bear Dance I saw performed at the Holiday Inn in Reno. Suddenly bears converged in that conference room as slot machines rang up pitiful gains and losses.

We joined the bear world as they danced for us, the same as we join the dancers spiraling from this lawn.

We have always been together.

☆

My son called me once at three in the morning. I could not sleep after the call, worrying for him and wondered once again about the wisdom of bringing children into the world who will suffer. A child's suffering always finds the most tender place in the heart, and a woman's children, though grown humans, will always be children.

Yet there's revelation in suffering, like the history in the song I heard the day after the call from a Plains group who performed on the lawn of the university.

Within that song was the beauty of horses. My son's name means lover of horses.

THE PLACE THE MUSICIAN BECAME A BEAR
FOR JIM PEPPER

I think of the lush stillness of the end of a world, sung into place by singers and the rattle of turtles in the dark morning.

When embers from the sacred middle are climbing out the other side of stars.

When the moon has stomp-danced with us from one horizon to the next, such a soft awakening.

Our souls imitate lights in the Milky Way. We've always known where to go to become ourselves again in the human comedy.

It's the how that baffles. A saxophone can complicate things.

You knew this, as do all musicians when the walk becomes a necessary dance to fuel the fool heart.

Or the single complicated human becomes a wave of humanness and forgets to be ashamed of making the wrong step.

I'm talking about an early morning in Brooklyn, the streets the color of ashes, do you see the connection?

It's not as if the stars forsake us. We forget about them. Or remake the pattern in a field of white crystal or of some other tricky fate.

We never mistook ourselves for anything but human.

The wings of the Milky Way lead back to the singers. And there's the saxophone again.

It's about rearranging the song to include the subway hiss under your feet in Brooklyn.

And the laugh of a bear who thought he was a human.

As he plays that tune again, the one about the wobble of the earth spinning so damned hard it hurts.

☆

I heard about Jim Pepper years before I finally met him in Brooklyn. He was quite a legend and appeared as a bear whose laughing could be heard all the way across this land.

He was a fine jazz saxophonist, constructing a music that included the tribal musics he heard as a boy taken by his father on the powwow circuit through Oklahoma as well as the more traditional elements of jazz. His mother is of the Muscogee people; his father was Kaw.

I've always believed us Creeks ("Creek" is the more common name for the Muscogee people) had something to do with the origins of jazz. After all, when the African peoples were forced here for slavery they were brought to the traditional lands of the Muscogee peoples. Of course there was interaction between Africans and Muscogees!

So it was not that strange for this particular Creek to pick up a saxophone and find his way to jazz.

I went to look him up when I began my study of saxophone and found a brother.

When he died I knew he had gone to the Milky Way, and had left us his gift of music—

I think about him at the stompdance when I see the fire climb, turn to stars.

Or when I walk the streets of New York and hear the music of the subways.

THE OTHER SIDE OF YELLOW TO BLUE

We cannot escape reckoning. We follow the yellow tracks, leading us
to the trickster who dives into earth and emerges in the music,
draped with afterbirth.

I don't ever want to lose the beauty of a horn, piano, bass following
the beat through impossible rooms of the bruised who try again for
sweet perfection.

The sky is the most obvious direction for saints. The rest of us enter
the back door, by way of taverns, lust or the smoke of something
religious.

Take yellow for instance as a drug. Something has to lead us to
winter.

The trickster in all of us thinks we can fool the judge, a tree bereft
of yellow who has no tears for the weary.

There's nothing we can do about it, except praise the ascent of yel-
low obsessed with blue.

Or sing of the miracle of destruction, like the four musicians spit out
by lions whose bodies turned to yellow stones.

*For weeks the tune "Contemplation" by McCoy Tyner lived with me.
Here's praise for McCoy Tyner, Joe Hendersen, Ron Carter and Elvin
Jones.*

THE FIELD OF MIRACLES

I spent a year saying good-bye and first perceived the field of miracles from the window of her apartment in Brooklyn. The flowers needed water and so did the people walking by underneath and I was always aware of the darkest loam; there a red leaf revealed the labyrinth.

In Pisa, Italy, it all came back to me: the leaf a codex for a season of memory. The nightmare of her childhood roared from a dream in which I carried her as a child from the destruction of her father, a place she guarded as the woman she is now, fifty years later. She then hated me for witnessing her shame, her face was a version of Picasso's "Guernica" and I left that dream with the child in my arms, laid her down next to me.

In the morning she had grown to womanhood, was drinking coffee in my living room. I don't know how she came to leave. I went to pour another cup of coffee, turned up the radio to dispel the outlines of the nightmare. She disappeared. I never did say good-bye.

Nothing prepares you for the Leaning Tower in the moonlight and it will always be the unanswered question in the field of miracles. The field of miracles is a question, as all the stunning marble beckons you toward history, the tower caught on the edge of some unseen boundary between then and now. There was some larger miracle in the shadow, as yet unspoken.

This is only one part of the riddle. The tower was a ghost under the raving sky, tilted toward paradise or was it leaning from some ruin? It will always exist outside any forced construct.

This poem is a construct but I opt for the structure of dreams, and still haven't solved the red leaf I turned over in my hand as we walked through the park, the northern hemisphere headed for winter, as if nothing ever happened in the dark.

Maybe that was the trigger, how I came to see the field of miracles. Or it was the mystery of bells startling me thoughout Italy, but I don't know the answer. It could all be some version of a word for good-bye.

Genova staggered north of there. Did Columbus say good-bye as he set off to test the limits of the edge of the world? What did he expect to find? The sea at night was a woman who had encountered the nightmare. Sea foam was her clay. She made stars and birds.

I could see Columbus and his teetering ships setting off with such bravado, the same bravado that created the Leaning Tower, that beat the child into womanhood. They sailed off the end of the world, though it has been recorded otherwise. What they found I will leave to another poem, though it is part of every story, the deepest loam, the veins of the red leaf I kept, a map to the field of miracles.

In the bowels of New York City I searched for the entrance to Port Authority, passed the coked-out beggars, the women without wings, and Helen with freckles, a feckless target for a burned-out hunter in the labyrinth.

The train must have leaped the tracks. For there in the strange loop, like a trick of memory turning rhythm and sound into birds and stars, was a band of Bolivian Indian musicians. I heard them first, in that park in Brooklyn as we picked up the leaf, from the Bridge of Sighs, and then here at the edge of the world the place Columbus brought with him, pulled behind him, the Leaning Tower caught on the undertow.

Against the gutted nightmare, the trains pounding through the labyrinth, the flute and drum took over. We were all revealed in the shame of forgetfulness as the mystery of the Americas fled from captivity.

And there she was as I turned up the music, filled her cup of coffee, in the field of miracles, where we are living and dying, making love and killing each other.

It's possible to understand the world from studying a leaf. You can comprehend the laws of aerodynamics, mathematics, poetry and biology through the complex beauty of such a perfect structure.

It's also possible to travel the whole globe and learn nothing.

PETROGLYPH

FOR JAUNE QUICK-TO-SEE SMITH

Everyone had turned off their televisions to watch the meteor shower flood midnight. Who named them Delta Aquarids? And what names were sealed on the lips of grandparents who'd slipped out of their disassembling bones, back onto resurrected horses, roaming the cities where there were no longer cities but cleansing wind threading the leaves?

In Corrales the horse named Sally knew what love was about when she lifted up her head to acknowledge the flying stars who were nodding to her, and to our humanness worn about us like rags in this war to survive with dignity. Even the chickens who had become too civilized clucked in assent in their dreams, the one place they remembered how to fly over the walls of chicken wire, their skirts forgotten, the pull of worms underground the rudder for perfect flight.

And dogs, the chosen companions for humans, had long since made their choice to stay, not out of pity but love. Rudy in particular danced around the feet of the painter who poured herself another cup of coffee before going outside to catch the blessing of stars that would suddenly light up the world.

Even though it was something the painter didn't think about (with words) she recalled the metallic flavor of minerals (how the stars must taste) scratching at the root of her tongue, which led to nerveways of the bones where the imprint of all symbols surface to the fingers, where horses ride through the colors needed to form any coherent universe. And never far away is the lightning of the heart that quickens the need to understand the night sky as a word which you can create in the same manner that you were created, as were the stars talked into painting our vision with promise of eternity.

Petroglyphs on a ridge of stones overlook Corrales. Everything is going on if you look close enough: a similar version of the pageant of whirling stars, arrows pointing to the sún, a child who has lost her way but will find it and the painter who stands out in the rain of horses where the night is always a puzzle of origins.

And how did she know that someone hadn't conceived of her, as they ran out of their house to watch the falling stars, light-years away (in the language of the enemy) but as close as the pulse in her wrist counting the surge of love?

As she stands outside the kitchen door, drawn by the whirling patterns of the electric stars, she can see herself painting the dawn as it elopes over the Sangre de Cristos, the crisp nostrils of Sally the horse snorting cool breaths into clouds, Rudy the collie dog brushing the ground with her tail as she anticipates the presence of the human she has chosen, forgetful chickens scratching for seed and the grandparents on horses with grandchildren in front of them, forming the border of ongoing composition.

Jaune Quick-To-See Smith's paintings are rich with levels of dream stuff intermixed with hard reality. The horse she keeps between her studio and home is always present in her canvases as well as her children and the history of her tribal people.

The land to the west of her house is rich in petroglyphs. The story they tell is still unfolding and appears at pertinent moments in her paintings.

I've always felt that Jaune constructs her paintings in a similar manner that I construct poems. She began creating first as a writer. I began as a painter.

FISHING

This is the longest day of the year, on the Illinois River or a similar river in the same place. Cicadas are part of the song as they praise their invisible ancestors while fish blinking back the relentless sun in Oklahoma circle in the muggy river of life. They dare the fisher to come and get them. Fish too anticipate the game of fishing. Their ancestors perfected the moves, sent down stories that appear as electrical impulses when sunlight hits water. The hook carries great symbology in the coming of age, and is crucial to the making of warriors. The greatest warriors are those who dangle a human for hours on a string, break sacred water for the profanity of air, then snap fiercely back into pearly molecules that describe fishness.

They smell me as I walk the banks with fishing pole, night crawlers and a promise I made to that old friend Louis to fish with him this summer. This is the only place I can keep that promise, inside a poem as familiar to him as the banks of his favorite fishing place. I try not to let the fish see me see them as they look for his tracks on the soft earth made of fossils and ashes. I hear the burble of fish talk: *When is that old Creek coming back? He was the one we loved to tease most, we liked his songs and once in a while he gave us a good run.*

Last night I dreamed I tried to die. I was going to look for Louis. It was rather comical. I worked hard to muster my last breath, then lay down in the summer, along the banks of the last mythic river, my pole and tackle box next to me. What I thought was my last breath floated off as a cloud making an umbrella of grief over my relatives. How embarrassing when the next breath came, and then the next. I reeled in one after another, as if I'd caught a bucket of suckers instead of bass. I guess it wasn't my time, I explained, and went fishing anyway as a liar and I know most fishers to be liars most of the time. Even Louis when it came to fishing, or even dying.

The leap between the sacred and profane is as thin as fishing line, and is part of the mystery on this river of life, as is the way our people continue to make warriors in the strangest of times. I save this part of the poem for the fish camp next to the oldest spirits whose dogs bark to greet visitors. It's near Louis's favorite spot, where the wisest and fattest fish laze. I'll meet him there.

☆

A few weeks before he died I wrote my friend the Muscogee poet, Louis Oliver, a promise that I would go fishing with him in Oklahoma that summer. Fishing to Louis was holy communion.

The struggle of the universe is exemplified in the sport. Yet it's possible to find the answer to every question with the right pole, the right place on the river.

As I mailed the letter I had a strange feeling the letter would never reach him. That cloud of illogic hovered over me for a few days.

When I was informed of his death I knew I had to keep that promise.

This is how I kept it.

PROMISE
FOR KRISTA RAE CHICO

The guardians of dusk blow fire from the Rincons as clouds confer over the Catalinas in the fading tracks of humans. I interpret the blur of red as female rain tomorrow, or the child born with the blessings of animals who will always protect her.

I am always amazed at the skill of rain clouds who outline the weave of human density. Crickets memorize the chance event with rain-songs they have practiced for centuries. I am re-created by that language. Their predictions are always true. And as beautiful as saguaro flowers drinking rain.

I see the moon as I have never seen the moon, a half-shell, just large enough for a cradleboard and the child who takes part in the dance of evolution as seen in the procession of tadpoles to humans painting the walls with wishes.

From the moon we all look the same.

In two days the girl will be born and nothing will ever look the same. I knew the monsoon clouds were talking about it as they softened the speed of light.

Cedar smoke in a prayer house constructed in the last century pervades my memory. Prayer lingers in the ancestral chain.

You can manipulate words to turn departure into aperture, but you cannot figure the velocity of love and how it enters every equation. It's related to the calculation of the speed of light, and how light prevails.

And then the evening star nods her head, nearby a lone jet ascending. I understand how light prevails. And when she was born it rained. Everything came true the way it was promised.

☆

The spring before my granddaughter Krista's birth I was a passenger on a plane approaching Tucson. We ran into rain clouds and were told to expect violent turbulence.

I knew the rain clouds loved us and it was with the knowledge of this love I was able to hear them.

They guided us gently down and I can still hear their voices.

When they guthered before Krista's birth I knew they were with us, blessing her.

THE DAWN APPEARS WITH BUTTERFLIES

You leave before daybreak to prepare your husband's body for burial at dawn. It is one of countless dawns since the first crack of consciousness, each buried in molecular memory, each as distinct as your face in the stew of human faces, your eyes blinking back force in the vortex of loss and heartbreak.

I put on another pot of coffee, watch out the kitchen window at the beginning of the world, follow your difficult journey to Flagstaff, through rocks that recall the scarlet promises of gods, their interminable journeys, and pine. Until I can no longer see, but continue to believe in the sun's promise to return:

And it will this morning. And tomorrow. And the day after tomorrow, building the spiral called eternity out of each sun, the dance of butterflies evoking the emerging.

Two nights ago you drove north from the hospital at Flagstaff, after his abandonment to the grace we pursue as wild horses the wind. Your grief was the dark outlining the stars. One star in particular waved to you as you maneuvered in the nightmare of the myth of death. It broke loose, stammered, then flew marking the place between the star house of the gods and Third Mesa.

You laughed with the spirit of your husband who would toss stars! And your tears made a pale butterfly, the color of dawn, which is the color of the sky of the next world, which isn't that far away.

There is no tear in the pattern. It is perfect, as our gradual return to the maker of butterflies, or our laughter as we considered the joke of burying him in the shirt you always wanted him to wear, a shirt he hated.

Someone is singing in the village. And the sacredness of all previous dawns resonates. That is the power of the singer who respects the power of the place without words, which is as butterflies, returning to the sun, our star in the scheme of stars, of revolving worlds.

And within that the power of the dying is to know when to make that perfect leap into everything. We are all dying together, though there is nothing like the loneliness of being the first or the last, and we all take that place with each other.

In the west at every twilight since the beginning, the oldest spirits camp out with their dogs. It is always in the season just before winter. It is always shooting star weather and they wash dishes by dipping them in river water warmed in a bucket.

Coffee heats over the fire. Crows take their sacred place. The sun always returns and butterflies are a memory of one loved like no other. All events in the universe are ordinary. Even miracles occur ordinarily as spirits travel to the moon, visit distant relatives, as always.

Then at dusk they share the fire that warms the world, and sit together remembering everything, recounting the matrix of allies and enemies, of sons and daughters, of lovers and lovers, each molecule of the sky and earth an explosion of memory within us.

In this fierce drama of everything we are at this juncture of our linked journey to the Milky Way—as your babies stir in bittersweet dreams while you travel to your most difficult good-bye—as Grandma lies down with them to comfort them—as your father's truck starts down the road in the village as a dog barks—

everything is a prayer for this journey.
As you shut the door behind you in the dark:

Wings of dusk
Wings of night sky
Wings of dawn
Wings of morning light

It is sunrise now.

☆

I was on my way to Tuba City, located in northern Arizona, the heart-
land of Hopi and Navajo country, and had decided to stop at Second
Mesa to see some friends of mine. Their daughter was going to partici-
pate for the first time in the Butterfly Dance.

I stopped at Rosanda's mother's, who told me Rosanda's husband had
died suddenly of a condition that had been in remission. He was a very
young man. Because he had so looked forward to his daughter's partici-
pation in the Butterfly Dance the family decided to go ahead with their
part in it. They knew that he would be able to see her anyway, that his
spirit was much like a butterfly.

I then found Rosanda and the rest of the family at the plaza with the
dancers.

The next few days unfolded with grief as well as laughter, as the family
prepared for the burial and release of this man who had lived respect-
fully, by telling stories, feeding people, by remembering him.

The afternoon before his burial Rosanda went to pick out the shirt in
which to bury him. She brought a couple into the living room to show
me.

"What do you think of this one?" she asked. "I bought this shirt for him three years ago. It's my favorite and he would never wear it."

We laughed, thinking of him wearing the shirt she loved, the shirt he refused to wear through eternity.

I'm sure he laughed with us. That's the way he was.

PERHAPS THE WORLD ENDS HERE

The world begins at a kitchen table. No matter what, we must eat to live.

The gifts of earth are brought and prepared, set on the table. So it has been since creation, and it will go on.

We chase chickens or dogs away from it. Babies teethe at the corners. They scrape their knees under it.

It is here that children are given instructions on what it means to be human. We make men at it, we make women.

At this table we gossip, recall enemies and the ghosts of lovers.

Our dreams drink coffee with us as they put their arms around our children. They laugh with us at our poor falling-down selves and as we put ourselves back together once again at the table.

This table has been a house in the rain, an umbrella in the sun.

Wars have begun and ended at this table. It is a place to hide in the shadow of terror. A place to celebrate the terrible victory.

We have given birth on this table, and have prepared our parents for burial here.

At this table we sing with joy, with sorrow. We pray of suffering and remorse. We give thanks.

Perhaps the world will end at the kitchen table, while we are laughing and crying, eating of the last sweet bite.

MVTO